The Customer Signs Your Pay Check

By **FRANK COOPER**

President, Frank Cooper Seminars

Frank Cooper Publishing Company
P.O. Box 2906, Everett, WA 98203
(206) 348-5533

First Printing, August, 1984
Second Printing, January, 1985
Third Printing, November, 1985
Fourth Printing, July, 1987

ISBN 0-917219-00-7

Manufactured in The United States of America

Dedication

This book is dedicated to the girl I married in 1957, the mother of our six children, my business partner, my traveling companion, my adviser, and the best friend I ever had, Arnene A. Cooper.

About the Author

Frank Cooper continues to reign as one of America's most wanted speakers. Bringing energy, excitement and inspiration to the platform he delights audiences as he makes them laugh, makes them think, makes them grow. His knowledge and experience continually astound those who listen. His actual experience includes being a migrant worker, unemployed laborer, journeyman printer, union leader, first-line supervisor, father of six children when he graduated magna cum laude from college, monthly stints as a "convict" in prison, author, publisher, consultant to the world's largest corporations, and a happy marriage dating back to 1957. He represents the near-perfect combination of speaking skills, knowledge and experience that audiences deserve. Again and again he dedicates himself to the needs of the people who will be listening to him. No exceptions to this rule! Frank says, "Today people need facts and how-to-do-it information, the nuts and bolts of success. They want ideas and a pattern for achievement that they can use right away."

For information regarding speeches and seminars, Frank Cooper may be reached at P.O. Box 2906 Everett, WA 98203 (206) 348-5533

CONTENTS

CONTENTS

1

Poise and Confidence in Customer Relations

Have you ever stopped to consider why your company hired YOU? They probably could have chosen someone else if they wanted to ... but they didn't! They saw personal traits in you that are important to the company's image, and they hired you to help present that image to the public.

When you were interviewed for your job, the person who made the decision to hire you was looking for specific personal qualities from among job applicants. Every business knows that its success in the marketplace can be greatly enhanced by hiring the "right" people. The "hiring decision" is one of the most expensive decisions that a company makes if you consider the cost of training a new employee, and the total amount of wages and benefits that will be paid during the total time of employment. But even more important is the question, "How will this new employee affect our customer relations?"

Key Concept #1: You, as an employee, are one of your company's most valuable assets.

When it comes to customer relations, your greatest strength will always be in the uniqueness of your personality. When you let your personality shine through you do a tremendous favor for your company. It makes people — customers — feel good about doing business with you. There really is magic in your personality! You have a personality that can not, and will not, ever be duplicated. And your unique personality carries with it your own special pattern for success in whatever you do in life.

The only thing necessary for letting the power of your personality shine through is to accept yourself and to like yourself. People who like themselves seem to have an easier time with whatever they do. They are the people who take a good look at themselves and decide that the only person they can ever be *is themselves,* and they learn to accept and appreciate who they are. They build on their strengths, rather than compensate for their weaknesses. They become themselves rather than trying to become someone else. And it feels good!

Now you'd think that this business of *liking yourself* might be pretty easy. Well it is for some people. People who were fortunate enough to have parents who kept telling them they were OK learned to believe in themselves early in life. But it seems that most of us picked up mistaken notions about ourselves early in life as our attention was drawn to our need for improvement. We grow up learning to identify our shortcomings much more easily than identifying our good qualities.

Another stumbling block to self-appreciation is the mistaken idea that we must be *perfect* at all times. Nobody is perfect! Each of us is OK, but not perfect. Life would be pretty dull if we all were perfect, wouldn't it? We must settle for being OK, realizing that we do make mistakes as we learn. Being imperfect is a sign of vitality, because it is a sign of growth potential, and growth is the only sign of life! If you are green you are growing, and if you are ripe you are rotting. Perfect is *ripe.*

When you make a mistake it is important that you take responsibility for the error immediately, rather than find excuses or try to "fix the blame" on someone or something else. The sooner you admit to a mistake, the sooner you profit by it, and the sooner you're happy again. Admit the mistake, correct it if you can, and get on with life.

Everyone has occasional experiences on the job that have negative effects on personal poise and self-confidence. It could be a corrective reprimand from the supervisor, a difficult customer, or some other uncomfortable situation that leaves us feeling "down." The temptation at these times might be to complain bitterly to fellow employees or to other customers, and this would be a mistake that could have significant negative results. When we complain, we sow the seeds of negativity in our work environment and when those negative seeds sprout and grow we find ourselves not enjoying life very much. We're much better off if we handle difficult situations in a positive manner, and then try to learn what kind of action can improve our future performance.

Remember, if you are conscientiously trying to do your best work, and trying to be the best person you can be, there is absolutely no reason why you should ever feel "second rate." The world's population is now in the billions, but among those billions there is not one person who is more important than you are. We're all in this together! When your poise and self-confidence get shaken, pick yourself up, brush yourself off, and get on with life. Handle reprimands and difficult customers as opportunities to learn more about people and life in general, and as a result you will discover that life gets easier.

And finally, don't you just love to be around people who like themselves? They're the kind of people who know that they are OK and don't have to go through life trying to prove it to themselves and to other people. Liking yourself is often a question of "Why not?" Who else can you be? You've got what it takes, and you don't have to add one thing to yourself. *You just have to let it happen!*

2 You Are A Customer, Too!

The best way to understand what goes into good customer relations is to pause for a moment and consider your own experience as a customer. You, the reader, are a customer almost every day of your life. How do you like to be treated when you are considering a purchase? What sort of attitude do you appreciate in a clerk or salesperson when it is *your money* that will be pushed across the counter in exchange for a product or service?

Can you recall a recent incident in which you were treated incorrectly as a customer? Is there a particular place where you resist doing business because *you just don't feel good about being there?*

As you read this book and learn the concepts of good customer relations, you will begin to develop a new perspective on every business transaction. In fact you will see living proof of this book's pages in your almost-daily experience as a customer. Examine these experiences as a customer and you will continue to develop a strong sense of what it takes to be successful in customer relations in the real world of business.

Key Concept #2: Use your own experience as a customer to help you understand the concepts of good customer relations.

As an employee, you have an excellent opportunity to enhance the quality of your own life by learning and applying the concepts of good customer relations. When you stop to consider the amount of time that you spend on the job, you realize that a significant portion of your lifetime is spent at your work! If the time you spend with customers is pleasant time, then your life is more enjoyable. Don't you agree?

There is a law that governs your success, no matter where you go, no matter what you do. It is called the Law of Cause and Effect. For every action there is an equal and opposite reaction. The Law of Cause and Effect applies to customer relations, too. When you take the time and effort to make a customer happy, you become happier yourself.

There are actually three legs to good customer relations. And just like a three-legged stool, if one of the legs is missing, the stool will topple. The successful employee is the person who gives diligent attention to each of these three components.

Key Concept #3: The three legs of customer relations are:
1. **The relationship that exists between the employee and the customer.**
2. **The relationship that exists between the employee and fellow employees.**
3. **The self-image of the employee.**

---

1. Customer Relations *is a relationship.* It is a bond or connection between two or more people, a bond during which people exchange attention and

communicate messages. Not all of the messages are communicated with *words*. Much of the communication is non-verbal and extra-verbal. The quality of this communication determines the quality of the relationship between the employee and the customer.

2. The relationship that exists among employees in a business is extremely important to the customer's impression of the business. Customers have an intuitive ability to pick up on how well people are getting along with one another at your place of business. It's not the sort of thing that the customer ponders and then reaches a logical conclusion about, but rather it is a *feeling* that the customer has. *And feelings are contagious!*

Perhaps you have had the experience of going into a store or restaurant where employees were not getting along with one another. What was the feeling that you had about being there, yourself? You probably would have been happier if the employees were happier.

3. Every person has a self-image, a mental picture of who he or she is. The mental picture begins to develop early in the person's life and continues to develop and change as the person discovers more about himself or herself. It is this self-image that dictates a person's behavior. It is as though a person's self-image becomes a *script* for that person to follow in any given situation.

Successful people have successful mental pictures of themselves, *and they simply act out their self-image on life's stage.* It is a well known fact that we become our thoughts about ourselves, and that a person who wants to improve his performance begins by developing a mental picture of himself as a high performer. This book will help you develop your own mental picture of the person who is successful at customer relations.

Employees who like themselves are said to have a positive self-image. I'm not speaking here of vanity, self-centeredness, or feelings of superiority. I'm speaking of the person who recognizes his or her own self-worth and feels comfortable with who he or she is, and most of all has reached a sense of self-acceptance. If you call to mind a particular person that you always enjoy visiting, chances are that same person has the kind of self-image we're discussing here. It is the same positive self-image that makes for good customer relations.

Across the nation a large number of businesses are failing every day. The number is staggering. The list of reasons for failure in business could probably fill several pages, but most of them would boil down to just one reason, *not enough customers!* Without enough customers, the lifeblood of any business is cut off.

The smartest businesses soon learn the importance of repeat business, which means that the company takes steps to make certain that the customer is happy enough to return for additional purchases, and happy enough to recommend the business to friends. For a business to succeed, its employees must realize that there is no such thing as a single sale. Every time a customer is satisfied, the likelihood for additional purchases is assured.

Key Concept #4: In the long run, repeat business depends upon customer satisfaction.

Here are some of the reasons why so much attention must be given to customer satisfaction.

1. The customer is the real reason that your company is in business in the first place. Every product and service is designed with the customer in mind.

2. It is the customer who will determine whether your business will prosper and grow. Your business may have dreams and plans for the future, but it will be the customer who determines whether those dreams come true.

3. The customer tells a business which products and services it can sell. People seldom buy things for which they have no need. The successful business must be keenly aware of customers' needs.

4. The customer pays every employee's wages, plus the rent, plus the utilities, and every other bill the business receives. Money is the life blood of every business, and every dollar it receives comes from the customer's pocket.

5. A satisfied customer is the most effective and least expensive form of advertising for the business. How many times have you purchased a product or service from a particular company because someone gave you an enthusiastic recommendation?

3

Ten Commandments
For
Customer Relations

1. THE CUSTOMER IS NEVER AN INTERRUPTION TO YOUR WORK.
The customer is your real reason for being in business. Chores can wait!

2. GREET EVERY CUSTOMER WITH A FRIENDLY SMILE.
Customers are people, and they like friendly contact. They usually return it.

3. CALL CUSTOMERS BY NAME.
Make a game of learning customers' names. See how many you can remember. This is a valuable habit.

4. REMEMBER—YOU ARE THE COMPANY!
In the customer's eyes, you are as important as the president of your company...probably even more so.

5. NEVER ARGUE WITH A CUSTOMER.

The customer is always right (in his own eyes). Be a good listener, agree with him where you can, and then do what you can to make him happy.

6. NEVER SAY, "I DON'T KNOW."

If you don't know the answer to a customer's question, say, "That's a good question. Let me find out for you."

7. REMEMBER THAT THE CUSTOMER PAYS YOUR WAGES.

Every dollar you earn comes from the customer's pocket. Treat him like the boss. He signs your pay check.

8. STATE THINGS IN A POSITIVE WAY.

Choose positive words when speaking to a customer. It takes practice, but it is a valuable habit that will help you become an effective communicator.

9. BRIGHTEN EVERY CUSTOMER'S DAY!

Make it a point to do something that brings a little sunshine into each customer's life, and soon you'll discover that your own life is happier and brighter!

10. GO THE EXTRA MILE!

Always do just a little more than the customer expects you to do. You will be richly rewarded for this habit.

The First Commandment for Customer Relations

The Customer is Never an Interruption to Your Work

*The customer is your real reason
for being in business.*

Chores can wait!

Most retail and service-related jobs include some responsibility for additional tasks, such as keeping your work area clean, straightening merchandise, and doing back-up work. These are chores that must be done by someone, and are generally part of the job description of the person who must also tend to the needs of customers. A retail or service business would not be considered successful if these extra chores were neglected.

Getting these additional tasks completed can become a problem in more ways than one. The employee who is responsible for doing the chores is likely to be scheduled for a specific number of hours during the shift, and at the same time be expected to complete all side-work. During times when business is especially good, and the company is serving a large number of customers, the frustration of having to do the additional work can create an uncomfortable situation for the employee who wants to do a good job.

As a customer, yourself, you may have had the experience of visiting a place of business where you intended to make a purchase. And as you entered the establishment, you noticed that the sales clerk was busily re-stocking merchandise or sweeping the floor ... and at the moment you caught his glance, a look of disappointment and exasperation came over his face as he "greeted" you. How did you feel as a customer during this experience? Chances are, you felt bothersome, and as though you came at the wrong time.

Customers don't like to feel as though they are intruding upon someone by showing up at the wrong time. Although the feeling the customer has might not be a strong feeling of embarrassment, he has a slight feeling similar to telephoning a friend right in the middle of his friend's family dinner.

When a customer is treated as though he is an interruption to your work, he feels as though he is not very important. In other words, when the message he gets is that he is an intrusion on chores, he tends to think the chores are more important than he is. And after all, you can't blame him for feeling this way if the employee looked sorry to see him.

Customers — because they are people — need to feel important. Customers must never get the impression that they are less important than other factors in your business. If a customer feels embarrassed because he thinks he visited your business at the wrong time he is likely to stay away from your business in the future. People do not like to go where they are not welcome.

Also, it is a good idea to remember that when your doors are open, *you are open for business!* Too often a customer will visit a business establishment ten or fifteen minutes before closing time, and the customer gets the impression he came at the wrong time because all the employees are involved in the work of closing up for the day. The message the customer gets is that he came to the establishment *after normal business hours,* and that he better not get serious about buying anything because it might create a problem.

Key Concept #5: There is never a "wrong" time to do business with a customer, when your doors are open for business!

Every business is created with one thought in mind, "Provide a needed product or service to customers!" The *customer* is the reason you are in business. Every chore, every task, every other activity must come second to serving the customer. Whenever the customer is put into the second position the business suffers.

Treat every customer as though you are really happy to see him, almost as though you had actually hoped he would come in today. Give him the impression that your reason for being there is to serve him, and you will help your business grow and prosper.

The Second Commandment for Customer Relations

Greet Every Customer with a Friendly Smile

Customers are people,
and they like friendly contact.
They usually return it.

Most of us understand the power of a smile, but too often it slips our mind. The smile is one of our world's most under-used sources of power. It can bring radiance and energy to virtually every situation. When we greet customers with a friendly smile, we nearly guarantee that serving them will be a positive experience.

Smiles are contagious! They spread faster than the common cold. As the song says, "When you're smiling, the whole world smiles with you!" If you would like to try an interesting experiment, and one that's easy to do, try this: Smile at the next five people you happen to meet — friends, family, anyone — and see what happens. Go ahead and do it. It'll be fun, and you will witness first-hand the positive power that you can have on people by simply taking the time to smile.

Some people don't know how to smile. They think that it is done with the teeth! And they couldn't be more mistaken. Perhaps you have seen someone with a smile on their mouth, and a bored expression in their eyes. Smiling is done *with the eyes!* And it is easy to do ... it requires fewer muscles than frowns do, about a third as many. You actually save energy when you smile instead of frowning.

Key Concept #6: When smiling at a customer, put the look of "I like you!" in your eyes. The rest of your face will then fall into place naturally.

Let's say that the typical customer walks into your place of business. The likelihood is that he has the ordinary "ups and downs" that we all have, and that life for him that day has been a mixture of pluses and minuses. Since most people consider themselves to be busy, he is probably preoccupied with the day's activities, and maybe even a little bit impatient. In order for you to get off on the right foot with this customer, it is going to be absolutely necessary for you to establish friendly contact with him as soon as you can, even if you are busy with another customer. Always make eye-contact with customers as soon as possible, and with a smile in your eyes that says, "Hello!" It only takes a second.

Customers have needs that go beyond your products and services. *They need to know that you know they exist!* No one likes to be ignored, and one of the finest ways to make customers feel important is to acknowledge their presence as soon as you can. This friendly acknowledgment will provide customers with the patience they need if there is going to be a short delay in service.

Employees, especially new ones, become overly concerned about how to greet a customer in a way that lets the customer know the employee is there to provide assistance. Some employers tell their help to say, "Can I help you?" and other employers say, "For goodness sakes — whatever you do — *don't* walk up to a customer and say, 'Can I help you?' The customer wants help or he wouldn't be here!" The best way to make a customer feel at home is to greet him as though he is a friend. After all, he is the most important friend your business has. If he is greeted in this manner, he'll probably let you know why he's there.

If a customer comes into a retail outlet, and says, "I'm just looking," let him look. Lookers become buyers if they aren't pushed too hard. Every customer has his own style of shopping. Some customers want lots of help and attention, while others do not. The important thing to remember is that every customer must feel comfortable at your place of business. You must be alert to "reading" the customer to determine what kind of shopper he is, *and then adapt to his pattern.* Don't try to make the customer fit into your own pattern ... it might not fit his style, and he'll become uncomfortable.

Key Concept #7: Customers must feel comfortable when doing business with you. Adapt to their style as best you can. Be alert, and be flexible in your approach to customers.

When customers bring friends or family members to your place of business it is important that each member of the party be acknowledged by a greeting, or at least by eye contact. Be especially nice to the children of customers. Giving them extra attention can pay big dividends. Not only will you be winning future customers for your business, but when children receive a lot of positive attention they seldom need to seek negative attention by "acting up." When children misbehave in a place of business it generally makes their parents feel uncomfortable, and eager to leave. Do what you can to make *everyone in the family* feel good about being there.

When the time comes for your customer to leave your place of business always remember to say "Goodbye" as though you were speaking to a friendly acquaintance whom you intend to see again. This farewell does not have to be a dramatic event, but it should make the customer feel as though he is always welcome. This last impression he receives will influence him in the future. People are motivated to return to places where they feel comfortable and where they have a sense of "belonging."

The Third Commandment for Customer Relations

Call Customers by Name

Make a game of learning customers' names. See how many you can remember each day. This is a valuable habit!

Have you ever had someone call you by name when you least expected it? Perhaps it was a time when you were walking down the street, or standing in an elevator, or walking into a place of business, and someone caught your glance and greeted you by using your name. How did it make you feel? Were you curious, interested, puzzled ... pleased? Well, one thing's for certain, the person who called you by name had your attention!

In today's busy, crowded, and sometimes hectic business environment more and more people demonstrate indifference toward one another. This can be easily demonstrated by walking down a busy street and observing passersby. Notice how many of them carry a blank expression on their faces, staring straight ahead, reluctant to look at other people. This is really a type of loneliness.

People really do have a need to *belong*. Each of us is motivated by a need to be accepted, and to eliminate loneliness from our lives. It feels good for us to be in a familiar surrounding, where people know us and call us by name. Some marvelous things happen inside us when we feel this sense of acceptance. We feel comfortable, we want to linger, we want to return to places that created good feelings in us.

You can be the kind of person who makes people — customers — feel good about visiting your place of business, because you call them by name when you greet them. You are probably thinking, "That would be fine, but it's not easy for me to remember names." Remembering names is easy, once you know how. You have what it takes to remember names. It's a simple matter of learning some simple rules for success.

I am going to tell you about four simple rules that will make it quick and easy for you to develop the skill of remembering names. You will notice that I call this a *skill*, not a *talent*. Imagine the fun that you will have, once you put this new skill to work for you. And the best thing about it is that you can begin today!

Key Concept #8: The four rules for remembering names are:
1. **You must *desire* to remember names.**
2. **You must *learn* the names you want to remember.**

3. You must *repeat* the names you want
   to remember.
4. You must *associate* the name with
   something.

Learning to Remember Names

1. Desire. Desire is a powerful motivator! It is that
seed of action that gets you moving toward the object
of your desire. Desire helps you take careful aim on
what you want, and impels you to action.

When you desire to remember names, you begin to
focus your attention on the *activity* of remembering
names. Without the desire, it will never happen. Right
now, you need to analyze your desire to remember
names. Is the desire strong enough to get you moving? If it is not, then picture yourself as the person
who has developed this valuable skill. Imagine the
first few times that you actually remember a
customer's name and greet that customer with a
friendly smile and call them by name. Imagine the
look of pleased surprise on their faces as they return
your attention. It will be fun!

2. Learn. The most obvious rule is that you must
learn the name if you are ever going to remember it.
This may sound simple, but how many times have
you been introduced to someone, and their name flew
right past you because you were not paying close
enough attention. You might have been preoccupied
with what you were going to say, or had given in to
some other distracting thought. It's perfectly normal
for us to do this and it happens quite often.

The *desire to remember names* will help you *learn* the names you want to remember. It will call for a conscious effort on your part. You must focus your attention on *getting the name* when you have the opportunity, either when introduced, or when it is placed on a sales order, or when the customer writes a check or pays with a credit card. These are all chances to learn the name.

If the name is not presented to you in any of the ways mentioned above, then you must *go after the name*. In other words, use your own effort to find out the customer's name. This can sometimes be accomplished by casually introducing yourself to the customer. It is important to do this without being too aggressive. Another way to get a customer's name is by asking the customer in a polite manner, or asking someone else who may know the customer.

As you learn the customer's name take a good look at the customer. Get a good complete impression of the person's features, coloring, height, and anything else that is distinctive or different about this person. Pay attention to what he looks like so that it will be easy to recognize him in the future. Remember, the customer may be wearing different clothing next time, so concentrate your attention on personal features.

3. Repeat. Repeat the customer's name. In a sense you will be *memorizing* the name as you repeat it to yourself. As you are talking to the customer, repeat the name in your own mind during pauses in the conversation or while the customer is looking at merchandise or involved in another activity in your place of business.

Another way to repeat the name of the customer is to work it into the conversation with the customer. "This is one of our most popular items, Mrs. Brown." "Anything for dessert, today, Mr. White?" "Thank you, Mrs. Black."

Whether you call customers by their first name or more formally by their last name preceded by a Mr., Ms. or Mrs. should be determined by what is likely to make the customer feel at ease. Adult customers seldom appreciate aggressive familiarity from young people, so unless an adult customer indicates the first-name approach, stick with the more formal. Since everyone wants respect, the safest approach with customers is to call them by their last name. It makes them feel more important, too.

Recite customers' names to yourself during the work day while you are doing chores like straightening merchandise or making your work area more tidy. Make a game of seeing how many names you can learn and recite in one day. You will be repeating the names and doing one more thing that adds interest to your job.

4. Associate. Associate the customer's name with some object or another person that will help you remember the name in the future. By associating the name in this manner you visualize the object *along with the person* on your next encounter. Your logical mind then *connects* the two together and you remember the name.

Associating the name is the creative part of the name-remembering process. And like all creative endeavors, there are no set rules or patterns to follow. You can come up with some pretty wild and off-beat objects, people or even places to associate a person's name with. Some of the associations will be flattering to the individual, and others will not. And if a person should ever ask you what you associate his name with, I would suggest that you refrain from mentioning unflattering name connections. I have learned this by experience ... uncomfortable experience.

As you *learn* a customer's name, study the name for a *meaning* or any obvious *connection to a thing.* Some names can be associated with characteristics that the person has, such as height, weight, coloring, hair, shape of body or posture. If the person's name is Mrs. Tower, associate the name with her height. If the person's name is Mr. Lightfoot, associate *Light-* with weight or coloring, and of course *-foot* with that part of the body. If the first name is Harry, associate it with the person's hair. In each case it is important to picture the person whose name you want to remember with the object you are using for association. In this way, next time you see the person you will also visualize the object of association. It works.

Some names can be readily associated with *places* and *things.* For instance, Mr. French can be associated with the country of France. Virginia can be associated with the state by the same name. Mrs. Fountaine can be linked with a fountain, and Frank can remind you of a hotdog.

Other names can be associated with occupations such as baker, cooper, smith and potter. The opportunity to associate names is almost unlimited. You can also associate a person whose name you want to remember with another person who has the same name. Perhaps the new acquaintance's name is Kathy, and she reminds you of your sister, Kathy. Once you make the link in your mind it will come back to you again in the future.

Some names will be associated with more than one object, such as the name Carson (car and son), Waterhouse (water and house), and Samuelson (sam and mule and son, or sun). These names lend themselves to the development of more complex mental pictures because they involve more than one item, but still the method works.

You will really have to get creative with some names such as Sattlemeier, Gerlach and Westling, but with a little practice Sattlemeier (saddle-in-my-ear), Gerlach (bear making Grrr sound as he tries to open a latch) and Westling (lingcod swimming westward) become easy to remember. Try it ... it's fun!

EXERCISE: Try your hand at associating the following names, using some of the guidelines mentioned earlier. Take your time and use your imagination. I think you will be surprised at how easy it is once you get started.

1. Brown _____
2. Bell _____
3. Kingshott _____
4. Tallman _____
5. Tackitt _____
6. Robin _____
7. Jack _____
8. Inkster _____
9. Nardinger _____

10. Rhodes _____
11. Holly Greenshield _____
12. Candy Hart _____
13. Frank Cooper _____
14. Bill Harryman _____
15. Ronald Moore _____
16. Amber Nichols _____
17. Mark Christianson _____
18. Dexter Lampers _____
19. Floyd Scanlan _____
20. Chester Krumsick _____

If you took the time to associate the names listed above, then you discovered that it becomes easier after you get started, and more fun as your creativity is taxed by names that are not readily associated.

Remembering names is a skill that can be developed easily and quickly if the simple rules are followed: DESIRE to remember names, LEARN the names you want to remember, REPEAT the names, and ASSOCIATE the names with other persons, places, things, occupations, or characteristics. Begin today!

7

The Fourth Commandment for Customer Relations

Remember — You Are the Company!

In the customer's eyes, you are as important as the president of your company ... probably even more so!

Retail and service businesses may be operated from virtually every imaginable sort of building, ranging from the tall richly appointed skyscraper to the lively shopping mall environment to the humble roadside stand. But without employees, a place of business would be nothing but a dull and lifeless building. A business is really *people* who are providing products, services, and sometimes ideas to *other people* who need them.

True, it is easier to succeed in a business that is properly located, actively advertised, and in an appropriately designed setting. These and other important considerations help to insure the prosperity of any business, but what gives *personality* to a business is the people who work there. The employees will be long remembered after a customer has forgotten the color of the paint on a store's walls.

It is important for all employees to take *genuine ownership* of their jobs, and to develop the feeling of "we" when discussing their business, rather than "they." Employees who identify strongly with their work are always happier on the job, and become the most valuable resource that any company has. These effective people realize that they spend a significant part of their time (Life!) on the job, and want to make the most of it. We feel sorry for employees who are *just putting in time* on the job, and are planning to start living at quitting time. These people are unhappy!

Key Concept #9: Develop a feeling of ownership for your job. It is your life while you are at work. Make the most of it. You will be happy and successful as a result.

There have been times when I visited retail and service outlets and was truly embarrassed for the owner of the business because of the attitudes of his employees. As I reflect on the source of my embarrassment, I realize it was because his employees didn't seem to care about the business at all, and their attitude was one of indifference toward the customers. The employees simply didn't care. It was obvious ... and it was sad.

On the other hand, I have visited businesses where the employees were enthusiastic about their company. They didn't see their jobs as work ... it was fun!

They loved their jobs and they found it easy to be successful in them. They were interested, lively, and enthusiastic. All this was made possible for them because they had decided to *become the business!* It was *their* job, *their* company.

When a customer visits your business, the most important impression he receives will be from the person who represents the business. He doesn't care who owns the company, nor does he care who your boss is. As far as he's concerned, *you are the company.* In his eyes, you are the most important person in the company, because you are the person who is going to help him fill his needs.

Also, employees who are well groomed and appropriately attired give the customer confidence in the business. He feels there is a "correctness" about the business. This is why dress codes and guidelines for personal appearance are important considerations for most businesses.

Personal taste in clothing is important to everyone, including employees, but in some cases and especially when an employee is representing the company, personal taste in clothing must yield to what's appropriate in the business setting. When employers enforce a dress code, they are correctly attempting to give the company the image it needs, and one that the customers expect.

The Fifth Commandment for Customer Relations

Never Argue with a Customer

The customer is always right (in his own eyes).

Be a good listener, agree with him where you can, and then do what you can to make him happy.

It is absolutely pointless to argue with a customer. The list of reasons why you should not is very long indeed. The list of reasons why you should argue doesn't exist! There is not one good thing to be gained by arguing with a customer, not even a "friendly argument," if you think there is such a thing.

When two people argue, they are really *fighting* with one another; it's just that they are using words instead of fists or weapons. This is why quarrels are destructive and always result in a situation that has been worsened by the argument.

The object of any business is to *serve* other people, and the quality of that service, along with the volume of service it provides will determine how successful the business will become. When customers get involved in an argument at a place of business, the result is *always* less business for that company. If the employee "wins" the argument, he is most likely to lose the customer. And the customer he has lost becomes an efficient form of negative advertising for the business. People don't forget arguments, especially if they lose the quarrel. A person who loses an argument, loses "face" and his ego is hurt. In order for him to get even, he must find a way to hurt your business. Maybe it shouldn't be that way, but that's the way it is with human nature.

Some people — employees and customers alike — like to argue with other people. I'm not certain why this is the case, but it probably has something to do with their upbringing or whether they like themselves or not. They will argue about *anything,* and in some cases it doesn't matter to them which side they take, they just want to argue. People like this are not much fun to be with, and seldom have many friends.

When you come in contact with a customer who seems to want to quarrel, remember that *it takes two people to argue.* When only one person argues, he is not *in* an argument, *he is simply complaining!* An argument is like a drama that has two roles to it. The decision you must make is to refuse to play the role of the second party to the argument.

The best way to handle a customer who seems to be looking for a quarrel is to agree with him where you can, listen to whatever else he says, and ask questions about his point of view. He will feel as though he is "educating" you, even though you realize that this is not the case. This will make the customer feel important, because he probably has very few listeners. It is also the kindest thing to do, and gives you one more reason to like yourself. After all, the thing that the customer wants to quarrel about seldom has any consequence on the quality of your life. And by listening, you might even be entertained ... and most certainly you will learn a little more about human nature!

When a customer has a complaint that involves your business, it is much different than the quarrels we mention above. Customer complaints must be handled quickly and as efficiently as possible. If we have a dissatisfied customer on our hands, we want the length of time that he is dissatisfied to be as short as possible. We also want that dissatisfaction eliminated — replaced with *satisfaction* — and certainly not add to his dissatisfaction!

Key Concept #10: Two things to remember when handling customer complaints: Handle the complaint quickly so the customer is dissatisfied for the *shortest* possible length of time, and don't do anything that will add to his dissatisfaction.

I believe that there is no such thing as a problem that does not have a solution, including the problems presented in customer complaints. But it can become frustrating when the solution to a customer's problem is outside our control. Let's face it, there are some problems that *we* can't do anything about. In some cases, our responsibility to the customer is not in *providing* the solution to his complaint, but in *finding* the solution.

If, for instance, the solution to a customer's complaint is outside the scope of your personal authority to resolve, then you must pass the problem up to the person who can solve the problem. This must be done as quickly as it can be *reasonably* done, and you must stay with the customer and his problem until you have accompanied them to the source of their solution. In doing this you will be letting the customer know that his complaint has not been dropped along the way, and you will not be adding to his frustration and dissatisfaction. Show him that you care.

When a customer complaint involves a request for refund, or the nature of the complaint will otherwise affect the income of your business, it is best to follow the policy of your employer concerning these matters. It is important that you *know* what your company's policies are in such matters in order that you be able to handle the complaints quickly. If you have done what you can for the customer, and he is still dissatisfied, then the best thing to do is to work at finding a solution elsewhere. True, it can become difficult, but you want that customer's business in the future ... and you also want to do business with his family and friends!

The Sixth Commandment for Customer Relations

Never Say, "I Don't Know."

If you don't know the answer to a customer's question, say, "That's a good question. Let me find out for you."

One of the most common and devastating mistakes that employees make in replying to a customer's question is found in the statement, "I don't know." When a question is answered in this manner, it is generally interpreted by the customer to mean, "I don't know, *and I don't care!*" It has a *final* sound about it, as though we have reached a dead-end in our discussion.

The habit of replying to a question with "I don't know" is generally formed in childhood as a suitable reply to a parent's inquiry. When parents ask children, "When are you going to get your work done?", "What time will you be home?", and "What happened?", the answer that requires the least amount of effort is, "I don't know." It also lightens the burden of responsibility, and allows us to avoid solving problems.

Customers become aggravated when their questions are answered with the illusive "I don't know." The reaction feeling in the customer is to say to the employee, "If you don't know, then find out! I want answers!" The saddest part of this situation is that in most cases the employee doesn't mean to be saying the wrong thing or frustrating the customer, it's just a habit, a slip of the tongue.

Now the fact is that a customer may ask an employee a question that the employee doesn't know the answer to. It's perfectly natural, and is to be expected in most businesses. The important point is that *there is no such thing as a question without an answer.* And it is the responsibility of the employee to provide the best possible service to the customer. It is for this reason that the employee must set out to satisfy the customer by indicating that the customer's question will receive the attention it deserves.

Key Concept #11: Every question a customer asks is a request for information that will help him make his buying decision, either now or in the future.

Always pursue the answer to a customer's question as quickly as possible. Let the customer know that he is important to your business and that his satisfaction is your priority.

If the customer's question is going to require information that is not readily available to you at the time of the inquiry, take the customer's name and how he can be reached with the answer, and always follow up by contacting the customer in a reasonable amount of time. Naturally, this idea of pursuing a customer's satisfaction by follow-up response to his inquiry is going to vary with the nature of your business and the type of question that is asked. Common sense must prevail.

When a customer is shopping at a retail outlet and can't find a specific item it is always a good idea to show the customer where the item is by taking the customer to the item. If it is in another department, turn the customer over to the appropriate person in that department, if possible. Although this is the ideal, it is not always possible to leave your station. The important thing to remember is that the customer must receive the attention he deserves.

10

*The Seventh Commandment for
Customer Relations*

Remember that the Customer Pays Your Wages

*Every dollar you earn comes
from the customer's pocket.*

Treat him like the boss. He signs your pay check.

If I were to ask you the question, "Who is your boss?", how would you answer the question? You would probably tell me who your supervisor or manager is, right? He's the person who makes many of the decisions about how the business is going to be run and he gives direction and guidance to his employees. Well actually, *the customer* fills that description, too.

Not only does the customer tell your business what products, services, and ideas he will buy, but he also decides whether your company will grow and prosper, and whether there will be a pay check waiting for you when payday rolls around. Every dollar you earn comes from the customer's pocket. The money may take an indirect route to your pocket, but if you were to trace its path, the trail would lead you to the customer. And it was the customer's decision to buy that sent the dollar on its way.

Too often employees see the customer as an *outsider*, a person who came in off the street and belongs somewhere else. When in fact the customer *belongs* in your business, and the more often the better. The customer is the key ingredient to your company's success, the same way a heart is essential to good health because it circulates blood to every vital part of the body. Money is the lifeblood of every business, and it is the customer who "pumps" the dollars to the vital parts of your business.

Money is a fascinating subject that is often misunderstood. Most people don't truly understand the process of earning money. The explanation is quite simple. In a free enterprise system of economics people exchange their products and services with one another. But instead of trading a bicycle for a filling in your tooth, or for your electric bill, you trade *money which represents your own products and services.* The only value that money has is in the products and services that it represents. If you couldn't buy products and services with it, it would be worthless paper. Incidentally, that's the best way to understand *inflation,* too. During inflationary times money buys fewer products and services than it did previously.

Most customers feel as though they worked hard for their money, and since they have a *limited* ability to earn money, they don't want to waste it. They want their money's worth. If they don't feel as though they're getting it, they'll spend their money where they'll feel better about it. You know that from your own experience as a customer.

Your company needs money in order to pay its light bill, rent, insurance, and the many requirements for keeping a business alive, including its most valuable resource, YOU! Good employees, and the way they treat customers, are at the top of the list for every business that wants to succeed. It's a simple matter of economics. Without customers, the business would starve to death.

Key Concept #12: Envision yourself asking the customer to sign your pay check, and you will develop an accurate picture of the customer's place in your own life.

Next time you serve a customer remember that he is making a decision about whether to buy, and how much to buy, not just today but tomorrow, too. Treat his purchase with the respect it deserves. After all, that purchase is paying your wages. The money doesn't come from anywhere else!

The Eighth Commandment for Customer Relations

State Things in a Positive Way

Choose positive words when speaking to a customer. It takes practice, but it is a valuable habit that will help you become an effective communicator.

When we communicate, we are exchanging ideas with another person. We are moving a thought from our head to the head of our listener, so that we and our listener are holding the same thought in our heads. Since everything begins with a thought — or idea — it is important that the thoughts we communicate be positive and constructive ideas.

Imagination does rule the world! As you look about the room in which you are sitting, you will notice that everything in the room began as an idea in somebody's mind; in fact the room itself began as an idea in somebody's mind. First, the person had the idea in mind, then developed a plan for producing the physical equivalent of the idea, then performed some productive actions ... and eventually produced the physical equivalent of the idea.

To understand how people communicate it is important to understand how people think. People think in words, pictures and feelings. While people think, they are actually saying words to themselves, and those words produce pictures in their minds. *As an experiment, try to picture something in your mind without saying the word to yourself first.*

As an illustration of the benefit of positive thinking, I would like to have you imagine that you have a "switch" in your head. The switch is called the PIRRAR Switch and has only two channels, Channel P and Channel N. "P" is for *positive* and "N" is for *negative.* The switch does not flutter back and forth between channels. It tends to remain on one channel or the other. Unless you know about this switch you are liable to let elements in the environment dictate which channel your own switch is on, and that would be a shame! Your thinking travels through this switch, and *thoughts become things.* The results you achieve in life will be determined by the quality of your thinking.

Key Concept #13: Positive thinking produces positive results!

Each of the letters in the word PIRRAR represents a word, and each word represents an activity that is part of your own thoughts-become-things process.

The letter "P" stands for the word *perceive.* We perceive our environment through the PIRRAR Switch. We see the world around us as being positive or negative, depending upon where our switch is.

Incidentally, we see in the environment primarily what we are looking for. For example, the person who wants to buy a house sees "for sale" signs as he drives down the street. The person who is not looking for a house seldom notices the signs. You can probably remember a time when you saw something in your own environment because you had been mentally focused on it.

The person who has his PIRRAR Switch on Channel P sees things in a positive way and is optimistic. The Channel P thinker begins to see *problems* as opportunities to succeed, and to realize that every adversity does carry the seed of a greater good. He knows that there is no such thing as a problem without a solution. He concentrates on solutions, but realistically recognizes that some solutions are outside his control. He knows that some customers are "problem people" and accepts that fact that he can't change people. He does his best, and gets on with life.

The letter "I" in the word PIRRAR represents the word *interpret.* We interpret the messages we get from people and other sources in our environment through the PIRRAR Switch. We either place a positive meaning on the messages or we place a negative meaning on them, depending upon where the switch is.

We hear what we need to hear, and anything that can be misunderstood *will be misunderstood!* This is particularly important to remember when dealing with customers. They will place their own meaning on what you say, depending upon what they *need* to hear you say. Perhaps you have had an experience whereby a person misunderstood you because he needed to hear you say something else.

As a motivational speaker, I talk to more than a hundred audiences every year. I know that every time I speak to a group of people virtually everyone in the audience will hear me say something that he needs to hear. I also know that in each audience at least one person will hear me say something that has a great deal of impact on that person's life. The humbling realization is, what they hear is not always what I mean!

It is important to note that when we communicate with a customer he will not always understand exactly what we mean, but there will be little evidence that this is the case ... unless a problem develops later. Then, of course the *problem* becomes an *opportunity* to satisfy the customer.

The first "R" in the word PIRRAR stands for the word *Record.* You have twelve billion cells in the memory portion of your brain, and every experience you've had is recorded on those cells, never to be erased. You carry with you, in your brain, every experience you've ever had. Some of the experiences are easy to recall, and for some reason others are more difficult to bring to mind, but they are all recorded there.

There are two reasons why your brain is designed as a recording device. The first reason is so that you will have a greater understanding of the world you live in. So that you recognize things in your environment and relate to them in such a way that you know what to expect from them. This knowledge helps you succeed in your environment.

The second reason for these recordings is found in the miracle of your imagination. You have a subconscious mind that sorts through all of these recordings whenever you have a problem to solve or are in need of inspiration. We have all had the experience of having an idea come from "out of the blue." This second reason is why goals are so important. Whenever you have a goal, this inspiration seeking device continually sorts through our past experiences for answers and ideas.

The positive thinker lays his switch over on Channel P and records his experiences as positive ones. As a result, the information that is stored in his brain is positive information. When he has a problem it is easier for him to see it as an opportunity because his solution will be drawn from positive information. The positive thinker gets positive ideas, and ideas become things. Every positive thing finds its beginning in a positive thought!

When experiences with customers are recorded in the brain as positive ones, the likelihood of positive success with later customers is insured. As opportunities arise to satisfy customers, the positive thinker has lots of great ideas upon which to draw. It makes sense, doesn't it!

The second "R" in the word PIRRAR represents the words, *Respond Internally.* By internal responses we mean feelings, or emotions. Emotions and feelings are the same thing, *they are mind-and-body responses to the environment.* When we encounter something in the environment the information is processed inside our brain and then mind-and-body changes take place within us so that we can respond appropriately to the environment.

Feelings are neither *good* nor *bad,* in the sense of whether you should be experiencing the feeling. Feelings are natural responses to our environment as we perceive it. A person who has never learned to fear an onrushing automobile may be indifferent or curious when he sees one coming toward him.

The positive thinker experiences more positive feelings than negative ones, therefore enjoys life more, and meets challenges with enthusiasm. The basic difference in positive feelings and negative feelings is this: We are set up mind-and-body to move toward and embrace the object of our positive feelings; and we set set up mind-and-body to either destroy or run away from things that trigger negative feelings in us.

It is easy for the positive thinker to be successful with customers because his feelings for the customer are positive. He has the *desire,* which is a positive feeling, to make the customer happy. There is a natural attraction between him and the customer, *because feelings are contagious.* Perhaps you have noticed how contagious positive enthusiasm is. The same is true for fear and anger.

The "A" in the word PIRRAR stands for the word *Act,* and stems quite naturally from feelings. Remember that *feelings* are a readiness to act in response to our environment. When we *act,* we are giving expression to our feelings. In other words we are producing the actual equivalent of our readiness to act. After we act-out the feeling, it is no longer within us. But the feeling will stay with us *if we don't act it out.* Sometimes we pick up a feeling in one environment and act-it-out in another, like the person who "has a bad day" at work and later vents his anger at home.

The positive thinker will act in a positive manner. This is especially important when considering customer relations. How an employee performs on the job is largely the sum total of his actions, and whether the actions are positive or negative will determine how he is perceived by his customers and by his employer. His actions will trigger feelings in other people.

The final "R" in the word PIRRAR represents the word *Reap.* We *reap the result of our actions.* That's the law of cause and effect ... for every action there is an opposite and equal reaction. As I say in the seminars, "The seed you sow will be the lawn you mow." It's an inescapable law.

For some unknown reason, a large number of people don't take the law of cause and effect seriously, when in fact it should be as obvious as "the nose on their face." The world is full of unhappy people who are trying to pound square pegs into round holes, and have never stopped to consider getting off what isn't working.

The law of cause and effect definitely applies to customer relations. If "happy customers" is the *effect* you want, the law says there must be a *cause* that can bring about the effect. Obviously, the *cause* must be a positive action.

The positive thinker must reap positive results, there is no other way. And that brings us back to our first consideration of the PIRRAR Switch. People are going to be successful in life to the extent that they monitor this switch they carry around in their head. Each of us has two abilities that come into play here. The first is our ability to monitor our thinking. Each of us has had the experience of listening to himself think. Our second ability is in a special gift our Creator used to set us apart from the rest of the world's creatures. That gift is called *free will.*

When we combine our free will and our ability to monitor our thinking we come up with the power to control our thinking. And when we take advantage of our ability to control our thinking, we take control of our destiny because *thoughts become things!* This success secret is not new. People have recognized it long before recorded history. You become what you think!

Key Concept #14: Form the habit of controlling your thinking. Lay your own PIRRAR Switch over on Channel P and you will:

PERCEIVE your own surroundings in a positive way. You'll recognize opportunity for happiness and success.

INTERPRET the messages you receive from your environment in a positive way. It's *good news!*

RECORD your experiences as positive ones, and you'll have a storehouse of positive information to help you make positive decisions, and from which you will receive positive ideas!

RESPOND INTERNALLY with positive emotions, and you will feel good about life much of the time.

ACT in a positive fashion, and the world will be a better place. You will soon develop the sort of positive charisma that sets you apart from the negative thinkers.

REAP the reward you deserve. Remember, for every positive seed you sow you will reap a positive harvest. It's the law of cause and effect!

Here is how to apply your understanding of the PIR-RAR Switch to the art of positive customer relations. There are three steps, and they all involve activities related to the switch. Lay your switch over on Channel P, and then:

1. Think in positive words. Remember, you think in words, pictures and feelings, and that imagination rules the world ... *thoughts become things.* See every customer encounter as an opportunity to be happy and successful during the time you spend with the customer.

2. Choose to speak in positive words. Use your free will and your ability to carefully select positive words in which to speak. Your words create pictures in your listener's mind. They can be positive or negative, depending on what you say. Remember, thoughts become things, and from positive thoughts must come positive things!

3. Hold other people in unconditional positive regard. Every person is special, just like you are! Some people are more difficult than others, but you must look beyond their lack of perfection, and you must speak to the good that is in every person. You will soon discover that when you treat customers and fellow employees as though they are important you enjoy life more. A good way to put this concept into practice is to concentrate on having people like themselves more as a result of speaking to you.

The Ninth Commandment for Customer Relations

Brighten Every Customer's Day

Make it a point to do something that brings a little sunshine into each customer's life, and soon you'll discover that your own life is happier and brighter!

Here's the secret of the Sunshine Boomerang! There is a wonderful and mysterious law that governs human relations, and in this case customer relations. It's called the Sunshine Boomerang Law, and it is a clear example of how the Law of Cause and Effect operates at the human relations level. The Law simply stated is this, *Whenever you brighten another person's life, the result is that you brighten your own!*

Key Concept #15: The Law of Cause and Effect as it applies to human relations guarantees that when one person makes another person happy, the happiness returns to the giver. It's called the Sunshine Boomerang Law.

Customer Relations affords each of us an excellent opportunity to brighten our own lives, and at the same time help our business prosper. Customer Relations is clearly a situation of *human relations.* It's a relationship between people. Just think of how much opportunity you have for a happier life yourself, by making each customer a happier person! The occasions for your own happiness are almost unlimited.

The world — *your world* — can be a better place if you take the small amount of time required to apply this marvelous principle of happiness. All you need to do is consciously sow the seeds of happiness in every customer you serve. Make it a point to have each customer think to himself, "Gee, I'm glad I spoke to that person," after they have spoken to you. If you keep this idea in mind as you deal with customers, it will soon become a habit that finds its way into other areas of your life as well. Without realizing it yourself, you will begin to develop the marvelous trait of *personal charisma,* and begin to stand out as someone special in the eyes of others.

To prove this Law of the Sunshine Boomerang to yourself, stop and call to mind a person who has been "special" to you. A person who made you feel important and as though you really counted for something. Chances are, it was a person who treated you with great respect, and it might have been when you were a child. Those impressions we receive as a child are significant to our discussion here. Every grown-up has a *little child* within himself. Sometimes the little child is hard to see because of the mask of seriousness that many adults wear ... but the child is there! I have yet to have an adult deny this when I speak on the topic during a seminar.

The little child in each of us believes what other people say about us, and no matter how well we mask our feelings, the way we are treated by other people always penetrates the mask and finds its way to the child. That is why we must never become involved in put-down jokes with other people. When we tease customers they may be smiling on the outside, but the little child inside doesn't like it, and it becomes a negative experience.

Key Concept #16: Put-down jokes that are designed to tease or entertain customers are never constructive to business, and nearly always result in negative experiences for the customer.

If you want to use humor with a customer, be certain that you are not using the customer as the topic of your hilarity. There are lots of other things to talk about. Another serious consideration here is the topic of off-color jokes or stories. Customers might politely laugh at them, but every person who hears such a story feels a little less respect for themselves, as well as for the person who tells the story.

The Tenth Commandment for Customer Relations

Go The Extra Mile!

Always do just a little more than the customer expects you to do. You will be richly rewarded for this habit.

Every customer who walks into your place of business has some expectations regarding the service he will receive and what will transpire while he is being served by your company. He develops these expectations in his mind as part of his decision to do business with you. It's a natural part of the process each of us uses when deciding upon future activity. If the customer's actual experience matches his expectations, he is a satisfied customer, and if his actual experience falls short of his expectations he is dissatisfied.

The secret of top notch customer relations is to always do just a little more than the customer expects. Surprise the customer by going the extra mile! He will then walk away from your business feeling as though he got more than he bargained for, and it follows logically that he will return to your business to satisfy his needs. He will also give your company the informal sort of endorsement that is such a powerful form of advertising.

Key Concept #17: By doing just a little more for the customer than he expects you to do, you develop the customer's loyalty to your business.

When businesses discover creative ways to provide a little extra service to customers they are richly rewarded for the effort. Usually the *little bit extra* requires very little effort or expense, and when measured against all that it takes to keep a business going can represent a wise investment in the future.

There is a logical cause-and-effect chain of events that form a success principle which can be applied to customer relations, and can guarantee prosperity in business. This *chain of events* can be visualized as seven dominos standing on end and lined up in a row. When the first domino is tipped over it strikes the succeeding domino which in turn strikes the next, forming a chain reaction that eventually topples all of the dominos.

Key Concept #18: The seven dominos for prosperity in business are: Desire, Goal, Inspiration, Creativity, Service, Success and Rewards.

---

1. Desire. Desire is a powerful motivator. When we *desire* to be outstanding in the area of customer relations, the second domino comes into focus.

2. Goal. As the result of *desire* for success with customers, we begin to formulate specific goals in our mind about how this desire can be satisfied.

3. Inspiration. Any time that we have a *goal* that is laced with *desire* it activates our own internal success mechanism, our subconscious mind, and as a result we begin to get ideas about how we can reach our *goal*.

4. Creativity. Once we begin to get ideas or inspiration in support of our goal, a marvelous little miracle occurs. The miracle is called *creativity*. Something new exists that did not exist before!

5. Service. Creativity is not creativity until it is given away! The object of creativity must be shared with others in such a way that their life is richer as a result. It must *serve* other people.

6. Success. Your business — any business — will be successful only to the extent that it serves other people. The more *service* your business provides to people, the more *successful* it must become.

7. Reward. The Law of Compensation, which states that for every action there must be a reaction, also states that every act of *service* must be *rewarded*. In our free enterprise system rewards take the form of money, the method by which we exchange goods and *services* with each other.

Key Concept #19: Businesses are not successful because they earn a lot of money. They earn a lot of money because they are successful, and their success is a result of serving customers.

The cause and effect pattern outlined above is a logical pathway to success in business, and can be followed by every company who wants to prosper. It took me quite some time to identify the "Seven Dominos of Success" but once I made this important discovery I knew I had a pattern that could be shared with others. In my own experience, I have seen this plan applied with overwhelming success, but there is one important key to remember! And without giving sufficient attention to this key, the formula will not work. The key idea is this: Set your desire on *service* rather than rewards, and your success will be guaranteed! The rewards will follow quite naturally.

If you ask yourself the question, "Who can I serve, how can I serve?", I feel confident that you will find the answer within your own business. And the answer to this important question will provide ideas that will lead to the sort of customer relations that can guarantee the prosperity of your company.

14

How to Handle Customer Complaints

One of the facts of life where business is concerned is the occasional irate customer who feels as though he has been mistreated or did not get what he paid for. No matter how diligently a company attempts to conduct its business in a correct fashion, customer complaints will arise from time to time. And it would be unfair to suggest that the business is always at fault when customer complaints do arise, but the question of *who is at fault* should not be the object of handling a customer complaint.

Key Concept #20: When handling a customer complaint, the question of who is at fault should never take precedence over resolving the complaint in favor of customer satisfaction.

The tendency in each of us is to "fix the blame." In other words, we tend to become defensive and find creative ways to convince others that it is not our fault when things go wrong. This business of fixing the blame does little to resolve conflict in a constructive manner, and is generally perceived as a waste of time.

Customer complaints must be viewed as *opportunities,* rather than *problems.* When a customer complains about a product or service it means that he is looking for some sort of satisfaction, and it is the *opportunity to provide that satisfaction* that the employee must give attention to. I believe this positive attitude will carry every employee to greater success in handling customer complaints. Look for the opportunity in every problem!

When a customer complains and does not receive the satisfaction he feels he is entitled to he will generally find satisfaction by other means. And he won't let up until he's satisfied, and maybe with a little extra satisfaction thrown in for good measure. The "satisfaction" we're talking about here is *negative* satisfaction and can take several forms, such as enhancing the story in his favor as he recounts the way he was treated by your business when the topic comes up among his friends and family, who incidentally repeat the story as their contribution to other conversations. Or perhaps the dissatisfied customer will write a nasty letter to owners of the company, the Better Business Bureau, the Letters to the Editor column of your newspaper, the Consumer Protection Division of your State's Attorney General's Office ... or Dear Abby. Let's face it, who needs that kind of negative advertisement!

Key Concept #21: The complaining customer will find satisfaction one way or another. The smart business makes every attempt to create positive satisfaction in customers rather than negative satisfaction.

It is not unusual to have customer complaints take an employee by surprise, and when this happens it can be a shocking experience that catches the employee off guard. Every job falls into a routine or pattern after awhile, and when this pattern is broken by confrontation with an angry customer it takes a few moments to shift gears mentally. When confronted by an angry customer it is important to *respond*, rather than *react*. By *respond* I mean the employee must take deliberate and measured steps to handle the customer complaint, rather than acting without thinking first.

The customer who returns to your place of business to "blow off steam" that has been accumulating prior to his visit has you as an employee at a significant disadvantage. The irate customer has been rehearsing in his mind exactly what he is going to say, what you will probably say, and how he is going to respond to what you say. It is as though he is prepared with a *script* as he begins to complain. The script generally does not work out exactly the way he thought it would, but sometimes he won't pay attention to that fact and he'll continue to argue long after it is no longer necessary. He just can't seem to let up until he's said it all!

A good way to envision the angry customer is to picture him as though he were a balloon blown up to nearly the bursting point. Imagine that as he begins to speak it is as though someone let go of the balloon and let it frantically flit around the room propelled by its compressed contents escaping from the balloon's vent. Irate customers are like that because you really need to let them blow off all the pressure that is built up before you can deal constructively with them. And after the pressure is gone you will discover a change for the better in their personality ... most of the time.

Key Concept #22: Seven steps for handling customer complaints:

1. **Listen attentively to everything the customer has to say.**

2. **Ask questions that help clarify your understanding of the situation and that let the customer know you are paying serious attention.**

3. **Propose a solution to the problem.**

4. **Ask if the customer would be satisfied with the solution.**

5. **If the solution is unsatisfactory to the customer, ask the customer what solution would be satisfactory.**

6. **If the customer's solution falls within the scope of company policy and/or you**

**have the authority to grant the solution
it is best to act on the solution as quickly
as possible.**

7. **If the customer's solution does not conform to company policy or is not within
your authority to grant, then explain the
situation and take whatever steps are required to at least try to satisfy the
customer.**

**1. Listen attentively to everything the
customer has to say.** It is important that you look at
the customer while he is talking to you, nodding occasionally as you listen to let him know that you are
following his conversation. Be a good listener and
don't interrupt him while he is speaking. Give him
every indication that you are interested in his problem. As you hear him out, give him plenty of opportunity to say it all.

**2. Ask questions that help clarify your under-
standing of the situation and that tell the
customer you were paying serious attention to
what he said.** If you listened carefully to what the
customer was saying you probably picked up a few
items in his conversation that you can ask questions
about. Asking questions not only clarifies your own
understanding and makes the customer feel important, but it also draws out the last little bit of steam
that might be inside the customer. The questions
should be aimed at clarifying the situation and should
avoid putting the customer on the defensive. The in-
quiries should be of a constructive nature.

There is no need for you to take the customer's anger personally. The customer really does need someone to talk to, and although he may appear to be directing his anger toward you it is his *frustration* that is creating the anger. It is not uncommon for young employees to make the mistake of letting irate customers ruin their day by taking things that customers say personally. As an employee, you are not there to get hurt.

You will begin to notice a change in most customers as you reach this point in handling the complaint. Generally customers become ready to handle the situation constructively once the anger is vented, and they are ready to do some listening.

3. Propose a solution to the problem. Generally speaking, an obvious solution to the customer's complaint will come to mind as a result of your listening, and it will be a solution that is acceptable to your business and to the customer. Smile and state your solution in a positive manner.

4. Ask if the customer would be satisfied with the solution. It is important to seek the customer's agreement on the solution. Smiling and nodding as you ask for his agreement enhances the likelihood of your success. If the customer appears to be satisfied with your solution, act upon it as quickly as possible. Remember, you want to minimize not only the dissatisfaction, but also the length of time it exists.

5. If the solution is unsatisfactory to the customer, ask the customer what solution would be satisfactory. If the discussion gets this far you may be surprised at what some people consider fair and equitable. While most people are reasonable, there are others who think they are entitled to much more than can be reasonably expected by way of repaying this "wrong" that has been inflicted upon them. Some people think that companies have unlimited supplies of money for the purpose of over-compensating the occasional mistake.

Let's hope that the customer's solution to the problem is reasonable, and will serve as a suitable alternative to your own suggestion. This is usually the case because most people seem to have a sense of what's fair.

6. If the customer's solution falls within the scope of company policy and/or you have the authority to grant the solution it is best to act on the solution as quickly as possible. Customers are more likely to be happy when they get *their* way about things. And when you take this extra step to insure that the customer is satisfied, you also enhance the likelihood of benefiting by the customer's future business.

7. If the customer's solution does not conform to company policy or is not within your authority to grant, then explain the situation and take whatever steps are required to at least try to satisfy the customer. There will be times when solutions to customer complaints do not come easily, and times when customer satisfaction can truly tax your creativity. But it is extremely important that every attempt be made to make a customer happy. There really is no such thing as a problem without a solution, but sometimes the solution is outside our control.

When you "run up against a brick wall" in your attempt to satisfy a customer's complaint, the best thing to do is level with the customer and tell him that you are perplexed by the situation. Let him know that you know how he feels about the situation and how much you wish that you could do something about it. Let him know that you care, and offer him a genuine apology. Sometimes there's not much more you can do than that. The important thing is that you reflect as much kindness as possible to him. Who knows, he may reconsider the situation in a few days and return with a smile on his face.

Customer Relations on the Telephone

No business would survive without the telephone. The telephone is a company's connecting lifeline to the outside world. Incoming and outgoing calls keep it in touch with its suppliers and customers. Telephone conversations *are* the next best thing to being there! Using the telephone is the best substitute for visiting the business in person, and how we use the telephone is extremely important to customer relations.

Businesses lose opportunities to serve customers whenever the customer is not handled properly on the telephone. We only have one opportunity to make a first impression on the customer, and often it is a telephone conversation that provides that valuable first impression. The customer will make some quick decisions about your business based upon how he feels about the contact he made on the telephone. The business who wisely cherishes the opportunity to make customers feel good pays diligent attention to every telephone call.

Let's begin with some ideas about how we answer the telephone. The most common mistake employees make in answering the phone is in speaking so fast that the customer can not really determine what has been said. When the telephone is answered, the employee's total attention must shift to the caller, and the standard greeting must be clear and at an easy-to-understand pace. When the greeting is mechanical and automatic the customer reads indifference in the voice of the person who answered the telephone and begins to feel as though your business doesn't care.

Have you ever stopped to consider that you can actually *smile* with your voice when you are talking on the telephone? That's right! If you're happy to be talking to the person who has called on the telephone your voice will have a warm and friendly sound to it. Your voice will actually carry a smile right through the telephone wire. When you do this when speaking to customers you make them feel glad that they called. It's good for business.

Key Concept #23: Always smile with your voice when talking to a customer on the telephone.

Incoming calls should be answered as promptly as possible so that the customer is not kept waiting. It is important that the telephone *not* be picked up while the employee is in the middle of a sentence that is part of a conversation with another person. When this happens the customer feels as though he is intruding, and he gets off on the wrong foot.

Key Concept #24: Always treat a customer's telephone call as if it were a personal visit to your business. Give all callers the courteous attention they deserve.

Sometimes an incoming call must be "put on hold" because the person who answered the telephone is handling a caller on another line. Always give the incoming caller an opportunity to respond to the question, "Can you please hold for a moment?" rather than cutting him off immediately. Sometimes the incoming caller may have a quick question that can be answered in less time than it takes to process a "hold call." If it is necessary to put a customer on hold always thank the customer for holding. It is best not to have customers wait on the telephone for more than one minute. If it appears as though the customer must wait longer it is a good idea to come back on the line and let the customer know, and to ask if it would be more convenient to the customer to have his call returned within a few minutes.

When talking to a customer on the telephone, never cover the mouthpiece in order to get involved with conversations not relevant to the caller's interest. The caller always feels subordinated under these circumstances. And *never* cover the mouthpiece and say something while the customer is talking on the telephone. Generally, the caller can hear and understand whatever is being said behind a covered mouthpiece.

Most of what applies to other aspects of good customer relations covered in this book also applies to telephone conversations with customers. Keep in mind that every time you talk to a customer you want to speak in a positive manner, brighten the customer's day, and provide the best possible service. If the customer gives his name, it is a good idea to use his name occasionally during the conversation. Calling him by name *personalizes* the call and helps give the customer some of the recognition he would get by visiting your business in person.

16

Understanding Human Nature

One of the greatest joys in working with the public is in learning to be successful with all kinds of people. This section of the book is meant to explain how people differ from one another, and how to be successful with various personality types. As we discuss some of these personality types you will begin to associate some of the types with people you already know.

It is true that no two customers are exactly alike. Every person is unique. But people do fall into patterns of behavior that become quite simple to identify once you know what to look for. And then the fun begins! Once you understand what makes people "tick" you have the key to becoming successful with them.

Key Concept #25: Understanding and working with the differences in people (customers) can become one of the most enjoyable aspects of any job that involves customer relations.

The first consideration when determining how to deal effectively with a customer is to make a quick decision about whether the person is an extravert or an introvert. The customer who is an extravert is outgoing and likes to make his presence known to those people around him. He thrives on involvement with other people and likes it when other people give him lots of attention. The extravert is interested in the world outside himself and how he affects it, so we want to be quite responsive to the extravert. He may have lots to say and needs a good listener, and because he is interested in the world outside himself the strong extravert may have more questions that need answers to satisfy curiosity.

The introvert customer is quite the opposite of the extravert. The introvert tends to be more private about his thoughts and feelings, and although he needs to know that he will get the service he deserves, he doesn't require as much attention as the extravert. He may have some questions, but they will be more thoughtful and designed to help him understand how a product or service meshes with his own *inner world.* The introvert customer is often misunderstood because he may appear to be unfriendly and aloof, and because he does not often demonstrate strong enthusiasm he may seem not to be an interested buyer. He's just different than the extravert because he's "incoming" rather than "outgoing." Treat the introvert in a low-key friendly manner because he is sizing-up both you and your business and will make a buying decision that is based on inner thoughts and feelings.

A person cannot be both an extravert and an introvert in the same moment, but can be more extraverted or introverted in different situations. You may be surprised to witness the generally introverted customer in a situation in which he seems quite outgoing such as a family gathering or sporting event. Every personality is a mixture of introversion and extraversion, although one of the patterns will tend to dominate. it will be more difficult to determine which is the dominant pattern with some customers because they are neither strongly introverted nor strongly extraverted, and with these people it is easier to match your approach with their personality because they are comfortable with both patterns.

If our discussion here helps you determine whether you are an extravert or an introvert, all the better! No matter which type you are, the key to your success with other people is found in acting in a way that is natural to you. You can be a friendly introvert as well as a friendly extravert, but the important thing to remember in customer relations is to *be friendly!* If you are a new employee, you are likely to act more introverted, while you are becoming familiar with your new surroundings. Once you become comfortable and confident in your new surroundings it will be easier for you to let your personality shine forth!

Key Concept #26: Extravert customers need strong interaction with employees, while introvert customers require a low-key thoughtful approach that satisfies their *inner needs.*

17

Four Customer Personality Types

In addition to determining whether a customer is an introvert or an extravert, we can put each customer into a specific personality type classification. According to Carl Jung, a famous psychologist, every personality falls into one of four basic groups or classifications. When we understand these classifications it becomes easier to deal effectively with each customer because personality type is the key to behavior.

According to the theory of personality types, people can be grouped according to these four classifications: Thinkers, Feelers, Sensers, and Intuiters. As in our discussion of introversion and extraversion, people are generally a mixture of the personality types, but one type will tend to dominate.

1. The Thinker Type. The thinker is a person who is extremely logical, and never makes up his mind until he feels as though he has enough information to be confident in the correctness of his decision. Once he has made up his mind he is slow to change it. Since the thinker seldom decides quickly, he may spend a lot of time shopping around before he makes a decision.

You can spot a thinker by observing his behavior. He likes lots of information that he can use to make logical and "correct" decisions. He will seriously weigh the benefits of any purchase against the amount of money spent on the purchase to make certain of its worth. One clue to the thinker type is that he likes to have things in a structured, orderly manner. He leads a structured, orderly life and gets frustrated if it becomes otherwise.

The best way to deal with the thinker is to present your product or service in a logical manner for his consideration. It has to make sense to him. The thinker does not like to be pushed or rushed for a decision, and will feel uncomfortable when this occurs. Once a thinker decides to do business with you he will continue to be your customer until it makes better sense to do business elsewhere. Thinkers like consistency in a product's appearance and want the kind of service they can depend upon. Roughly twenty-five per cent of our population are thinkers.

2. The Feeler Type. The feeler is a person who makes decisions according to his *feelings*. The feeler will decide in favor of things that arouse pleasant feelings rather than unpleasant, beautiful rather than ugly, exciting rather than dull. While the feeler is quite capable of using logic to make a decision, logic often takes a back seat to *enjoyment*. The feeler likes colorful items, cozy environments, the latest fad or fashion, and doing business in a friendly environment.

You can identify a customer as a feeler by watching how he acts and listening to what he says. When making a decision, the feeler may appear to be a little uncertain until he has the agreement of others, rather than risk the *bad feelings* that disagreements can bring. It is not unusual for the feeler to change his mind after a purchase is made, because when he took the item home he had a different *feeling* about it. The feeler's vocabulary is usually laced with words that describe things according to feeling.

To be effective with the feeler type customer it is important to present your product or service in a way that arouses pleasant feelings in the buyer. Feelers love to hear compliments, and being accepted by other people is extremely important to their sense of well-being. The feeler is generally not in a hurry to buy an item until he feels right about it, and may need a little reassurance from the seller. The seller should emphasize the pleasure that will come with the purchase.

Note: Feelers are generally quite pleasant to have as customers if they receive the attention they deserve, and they also become extremely loyal to their favorite business establishments. But a feeler once angered can be hard to get back as a customer. About twenty-five per cent of all people are feelers.

3. The Senser Type. Unlike the thinker and the feeler who must ponder decisions in order to sort out the logic and to examine feelings, the senser is a "right now" individual whose mind seems already made up based on the sensory data at hand. The senser may appear to be impulsive, but does not need to know *why* so much as he needs to *act* and get on with things. He is more interested in practicality than he is logic and beauty.

You can spot the senser customer because he is quick to decide and quick to act. If he is shopping for an item he will give your item choices a quick examination and select one that will do the job, pay for it, and leave. And if the senser stands in line to pay for his purchase he might pick up one or two impulse items that catch his eye. The senser does not shop around from store to store for the best deal because he's simply not interested in making detailed comparisons. With a little imagination you can see how the senser customer might respond to your own business, no matter what the product or service is.

The best way to handle the senser customer is to use the direct approach. Give him what he wants, because the likelihood of being able to "sell" him something is not great. If the senser is making a choice that he may be unhappy with later, you can point out the practical aspects of an alternate choice and if the customer *senses* that your observations are correct he will quickly change his mind and be on his way.

Like all other customers, the senser likes courteous service, but also appreciates service that is quick. The senser is a *convenience* shopper who will become a regular customer if doing business with you is not complicated. About forty percent of us are sensers.

4. The Intuiter Type. Like the senser, the intuiter is quick to make up his mind and may appear to be an impulsive person. The intuiter does not ponder decisions, but instead acts upon "hunch" or intuition. The intuiter seems to have an inborn sense about things and does not need to gather much information in order to make a decision. The intuiter is often futuristic and creative, and usually has a feeling about "what's coming next."

As a customer, the intuiter will be the most challenging type to figure out. There's very little about the intuiter's behavior that can tip you off to his type. The intuiter does not like to get bogged down with detail and may tend to be a little disorganized. Because the intuiter is often future-oriented he is interested in whatever is new and different. The intuiter customer is less likely to fall into patterns of behavior such as shopping at the same place, going to the same restaurant, or developing a strong loyalty to any one place of business.

The best way to handle the intuiter is to listen carefully to what he says he is looking for, and to present him with whatever products and services might match his vision. You may also wish to point out products and services that are new to your business, and to let him know what's coming in the future. The intuiter may provide important tips to your business about products and services that will be in demand in the near future. Ask the intuiter lots of questions, and you'll be surprised what you can learn! About ten percent of us are intuiters.

Important: Each of us is a mixture of the four personality types discussed here, but in most of us one of the types seems to dominate. It should be noted that each of the types has its strengths and weaknesses, and that none of the types are either good or bad.

Key Concept #27: There are four basic personality types: Thinker, Feeler, Senser, and Intuiter. In the role of customer, each type is distinctly different from the others.

18

Three Roles Customers Play

It's been said that life is a stage and each of us selects a role to play. Students of human nature identify three basic roles that people play, especially during times of conflict. Your understanding of these roles and their relationship to one another will be helpful in handling customer complaints, and in dealing effectively with difficult people. In a nutshell, the three roles are *the persecutor, the victim, and the rescuer.*

I'd like to have you stop and think about a drama that really held your interest. It could be a movie, a television show, or a good book. In each case it would be quite easy to assign each of the roles — persecutor, victim, rescuer — to various players in the cast. And it was the way in which these roles *changed* that held your interest and provided the sense of drama that entertained you. Subconsciously, you had a "happy ending' in mind for the drama which involved a final shift of the roles to where you wanted them to be. You wanted the persecutor to finally become the victim, the victim to experience justice, and the rescuer to be successful in his efforts.

Key Concept #28: The three basic drama roles customers play during times of conflict are: Persecutor, Victim, or Rescuer.

---

1. The Persecutor. We understand the word *persecute* to mean the act of oppressing or harassing another person. Sometimes people appear to have a *need* to persecute others, and look for opportunities to do so. In order to find this opportunity to persecute it is often necessary for them to develop a situation whereby they can become the persecutor. Because the act of persecution in this case is based on a psychological need the persecutor has, it is often hard to understand why he is so upset over such a seemingly trivial matter. The person who needs to persecute wants to manipulate someone else into the *victim* role.

The manipulative persecutor customer might be the customer who becomes quite angry if he believes that service is slow, or the customer who makes a scene in a restaurant because there was a mistake in his order, or the customer who purchases a defective item and wants to have a letter about your "lousy merchandise" published in the local newspaper. Let's face it, some people just seem to need to pick on others. Usually it is because they have had a "bad day" and things don't seem to be going right for them. As a result the persecutor looks for someone to dump his bad feelings on.

The best way to handle the persecutor is to recognize him as such, and to refuse to assume the victim role to the extent of having it affect your feelings about yourself and your job. Remember, the persecutor is a "problem looking for someplace to happen!" Do whatever you can to satisfy the persecutor, but don't take his hostility personally. Let his mean words roll off like water on a duck's back. Deal with him in a direct and courteous manner, but don't be "sticky sweet" with him or you will irritate him further.

2. The Victim. In the drama of customer dissatisfaction the role of *victim* can often enter the picture. Ordinarily we understand the word *victim* to mean "one who was subjected to suffering." It is interesting to note that some people actually choose the victim role as their favorite role in life, and look for opportunities to become a victim. In order to be successful in becoming a victim it is often necessary for the player of the role to manipulate another person or group of people into the *persecutor* role. Remember, people who play this role *need* to be a victim, and are on the lookout for opportunities to fill that need. They can cleverly create situations in which they can "suffer" because of another person's actions.

In addition to manipulating other people into the *persecutor* role, the illegitimate victim may also wish to put people into the *rescuer* role. The roles we are discussing here — persecutor, victim, rescuer — are based on psychological needs that the players have, and the victim might be starving for attention.

As a customer, the victim actually likes to be in situations in which he gets to suffer a little bit, and when the need arises will create a situation in which he gets to fill that need. It might be the person who is careless in selecting shoe sizes or styles, and gets to bring them back to the shoe store later. It could be the person who gets to "suffer through" a steak dinner in which the meat was not cooked as he wished. As you picture these situations in your mind, you can begin to see the drama unfold as the victim manipulates another person into the persecutor or rescuer role.

Sometimes the *victim* switches roles to *persecutor* or *rescuer* as the drama begins to unfold. You will recall from our earlier discussion that it is in the changing of these roles that the actual drama takes place. The victim customer may wish to become the persecutor, and to manipulate the employee into the victim role.

The best way to handle the customer who appears to be playing the victim role is to give him plenty of attention, and to apologize profusely. You as a salesperson may wonder how the customer could have gotten himself into a situation of so much discomfort unnecessarily, but you must remember that for some unknown reason the customer *needed* to do so. The customer is blind to the pattern of his actions in this case. Do what you can to make the customer satisfied, and take steps in the future to make certain this customer does not victimize himself again at your expense.

If the victim-playing customer wants you to play the role of persecutor or to become the victim it is wise to "stand outside the drama" and handle the situation in a *professional* manner without getting your personal feelings involved.

3. The Rescuer. The third, and most subtle of the life drama roles is the role of *rescuer.* The rescuer role is played by people who need to be needed. In customer relations the rescuer role is played more often by employees than by customers, simply by the nature of business. The person who *needs* to play rescuer works at creating situations in which he gets to come to the rescue of other people, and finds satisfaction in having other people depend upon him.

As a customer, the rescuer-type person will want to give you a hand wherever possible. He may want to give you unsolicited recommendations for improving your business, or may personally escort other people to your business and make known the fact while doing so. The rescuer-type person is often a sensitive individual who can get his feelings hurt as the tables turn and he switches to the victim role as he plays "All I was trying to do was help."

The rescuer customer can be fun to have around, provided he does not get in the way and become an obstacle to the service of others. Here again, it is wise to give the rescuer all the attention he craves, but beware of the rescuer's tendency to move to the victim role for a different type of attention.

How Customers View Themselves

The customer's self-image — how he views himself — is an especially important consideration when it comes to customer relations. It can be said that customers hold one of four basic points of view regarding themselves in relationship to other people. It is this *relative* point of view that sets the tone of the *relationship* between you and the customer, and it is determined by a feeling of what we will call "OK-ness."

For the sake of our discussion here, we will use the word "OK-ness" to mean feelings of confidence and self-acceptance. The "OK" person likes himself and feels comfortable with who he is. He is satisfied with being himself, even though he realizes he is not perfect.

Key Concept #29: The four basic life positions that customers hold in relationship to other people are:

1. I'm Not OK — You're OK
2. I'm Not OK — You're Not OK
3. I'm OK — You're Not OK
4. I'm OK — You're OK

---

1. I'm Not OK — You're OK. This position in life is often referred to as the *inferiority complex position,* and stems from the person's idea that his own self-worth is somewhat inferior to the self-worth of other people. This person believes that his attitudes, ideas, opinions and behavior must be shaped to gain the acceptance of other people. He bases his image of himself on the smiles and frowns of other people. If people are smiling at him he's OK, if they're frowning at him he'd better shape up and adapt to meet their approval.

It should be noted here that every person occupies the inferiority complex position during early childhood — perhaps the first two years of life. During the first two years of life we cannot understand what words mean, we are incapable of logic, we're small in size and generally rely on other people to come to our rescue when things go wrong. As infants we enjoy feeling OK, but we rely on the "big people" in our life to help us feel OK and they become an important source of our OK-ness. In fact, that's how they train us: If we want to feel OK we do what we're supposed to do. If we do something we're not supposed to do the "big people" take away our OK feelings. So early in life we learn to base our personal success on the smiles and frowns of other people ... it's inescapable.

Some grown-ups never grow out of this inferiority complex, and some of these inferior feeling adults are your customers. You can spot a person who has an inferiority complex by the way he acts. He may be the person who is the bragger who needs to impress people during every conversation. He may be the person who dresses in a sloppy manner and is careless about personal appearance as a way to advertise his inferiority.

The best way to handle the customer who has an inferiority complex is to go out of your way to make him feel accepted for who he is. Make him feel good about himself with sincere compliments and respect. Bear in mind that the person who has an inferiority complex feels miserable when he feels his behavior is not winning the approval of other people. Because this customer seeks approval he will return to places of business where he feels accepted and OK. Go out of your way to make him feel important even when he's bragging or acting inferior.

2. I'm Not OK — You're Not OK. This person can be said to occupy the *cynical life position*. He doesn't like himself, nor does he like other people. He developed this attitude early in his life when he started to do a few things for himself and began to understand what words meant *IF* he had the kind of parents who did not demonstrate much affection toward him *AND* were always providing him with bad feelings in an attempt to get him to do what he was supposed to do. Early in life he made the decision, "I know I'm not OK, but you aren't too nice either!" Some people grow into adulthood occupying this *I'm Not OK — You're Not OK* life position.

It's easy to spot customers who have adopted this *I'm Not OK — You're Not OK* life script. They are the people who are negative about everything. They tend to complain every time they say something, and seldom trust people with whom they are doing business.

The key to effectiveness with the cynical customer is to not let him affect your behavior and the feelings you have about yourself. There is very little you can do or say to change this person's attitude about himself and other people, except to provide him with excellent service that is prompt and courteous. If enough people treat him this way, his inescapable decision will someday be, "I guess some people are OK."

It should be noted that there are two parts in each of the life scripts we are discussing here. The first part belongs to the person himself, and the second part belongs (from his own point of view) to virtually everyone else he encounters. The person who occupies the cynical position is often capable of projecting the Not-OK part of the script onto the person to whom he is speaking, especially young people who have fresh in their minds the adult-child relationships of their recent past. It's a good idea to make an extra effort to refuse ownership of these Not-OK feelings about yourself. Do your best at all times, and be assured that you alone decide your self-worth.

3. I'm OK — You're Not OK. This is said to be the *criminal* life position because people who occupy this life position have very little regard for other people. The holder of the criminal position usually comes from a family situation in which he was physically abused as a child. As a youngster, he already occupied the *I'm Not OK — You're Not OK* position as outlined above, but then later decided that if he was going to survive in his world he had better look out for "number one," himself. He grew into adulthood as the selfish person who had very little respect for other people.

As a customer the *I'm OK — You're Not OK* will be nice to you as long as there is a direct payoff to him for doing so. When the payoff is no longer there he shifts his attention to other people and situations that can enhance his life. This customer is usually easy enough to do business with, provided he receives excellent service and *always* feels as though he is getting a good bargain. He loves it when he receives special attention and believes that he is given favored treatment that others do not receive. If he feels as though he has been neglected as a customer he is quick to set friendship and loyalty aside and to do whatever is necessary to receive his own satisfaction.

It is especially important for your business to treat the *I'm OK — You're Not OK* person with extra kindness. This customer has few — if any — friends, and has little opportunity to experience the joy of loving relationships. The world becomes a better place when this person is treated with compassion, and you and your business will have one more reason to be proud of yourselves when you overlook the blemish on this customer's personality.

One word of caution: The *I'm OK — You're Not OK* person generally believes that he is right and you are wrong if there is a disagreement between the two of you, and will act as though there is no question about his correctness. Agree with him where you can, try to keep him satisfied, and go on about your business. But don't let his incorrect attitude ruin your day.

4. I'm OK — You're OK. This is considered to be

the *healthy* position in life, and is the foundation for all success in customer relations. The person who occupies this life position as a basic life script recognizes his own personal worth as well as that of others. He knows that he isn't perfect, and has grown to accept himself as he is. He tries to do well in whatever he does because he has respect for himself and wants to feel good about himself. He sees other people as being very much like himself, so he accepts them, too.

The person who occupies this healthy *I'm OK — You're OK* life script as his own personal style has made a decision about himself and other people. The decision goes something like this, "The only person I can ever be is myself. I guess I'm as OK as anyone is, so I may as well be a friend to myself and do what I can to have a happy life!" This person also wants other people to experience the joy and peace of mind that comes with such a decision, and treats others with the kind of respect that gives them personal encouragement.

As a customer, the person who occupies the *I'm OK — You're OK* position is a delight to work with. He doesn't get upset over small matters and realizes that everyone makes mistakes occasionally. If he has a problem with your product or service he is quick to understand how those things happen, and is more interested in resolving the situation in a quick and friendly manner. He wants to be fair, and expects to be treated with fairness.

The employee who occupies the *I'm OK — You're OK* position is a valuable asset to his employer as well as to the customer. It is easy for this employee to be service-oriented and to give customers the kind of attention they deserve. The positive healthy self-image of a company's employees can do more to insure the success of a business than virtually any other asset. If we were to list the benefits associated with positive employee self-images it could fill a volume and be titled, "How to Succeed in a Customer Oriented Business!"

Key Concept #30: The foundation for all successful customer relations is in the *I'm OK — You're OK* attitude toward people.

Key Concept Review

1. You, as an employee, are one of your company's most valuable assets.
2. Use your own experience as a customer to help you understand the concepts of good customer relations.
3. The three legs of customer relations are:
   1. The relationship that exists between the employee and the customer.
   2. The relationship that exists between the employee and fellow employees.
   3. The self-image of the employee.
4. In the long run, repeat business depends upon customer satisfaction.
5. There is never a "wrong" time to do business with a customer, when your doors are open for business!
6. When smiling at a customer, put the look of "I like you!" in your eyes. The rest of your face will then fall into place naturally.
7. Customers must feel comfortable when doing business with you. Adapt to their style as best you can. Be alert, and be flexible in your approach to customers.

8. The four rules for remembering names are:
   1. You must *desire* to remember names.
   2. You must *learn* the names you want to remember.
   3. You must *repeat* the names you want to remember.
   4. You must *associate* the name with something.
9. Develop a feeling of ownership for your job. It is your life while you are at work. Make the most of it. You will be happy and successful as a result.
10. Two things to remember when handling customer complaints: Handle the complaint quickly so the customer is dissatisfied for the *shortest* possible length of time, and don't do anything that will add to his dissatisfaction.
11. Every question a customer asks is a request for information that will help him make his buying decision, either now or in the future.
12. Envision yourself asking the customer to sign your pay check, and you will develop an accurate picture of the customer's place in your own life.
13. Positive thinking produces positive results!
14. Form the habit of controlling your thinking. Lay your own PIRRAR Switch over on Channel P and you will:

    PERCEIVE your own surroundings in a positive way. You'll recognize opportunity for happiness and success.

    INTERPRET the messages you receive from your environment in a positive way. It's good news!

    RECORD your experiences as positive ones, and

you'll have a storehouse of positive information to help you make positive decisions, and from which you will receive positive ideas!

RESPOND INTERNALLY with positive emotions, and you will feel good about life much of the time.

ACT in a positive fashion, and the world will be a better place. You will soon develop the sort of positive charisma that sets you apart from the negative thinkers.

REAP the reward you deserve. Remember, for every positive seed you sow you will reap a positive harvest. It's the law of cause and effect!

15. The Law of Cause and Effect as it applies to human relations guarantees that when one person makes another person happy, the happiness returns to the giver. It's called the Sunshine Boomerang Law.

16. Put-down jokes that are designed to tease or entertain customers are never constructive to business, and nearly always result in negative experiences for the customer.

17. By doing just a little more for the customer than he expects you to do, you develop the customer's loyalty to your business.

18. The seven dominos for prosperity in business are: Desire, Goal, Inspiration, Creativity, Service, Success and Rewards.

19. Businesses are not successful because they earn a lot of money. They earn a lot of money because they are successful, and their success is a result of serving customers.

20. When handling a customer complaint, the question of who is at fault should never take precedence over resolving the complaint in favor of customer satisfaction.
21. The complaining customer will find satisfaction one way or another The smart business makes every attempt to create positive satisfaction in customers rather than negative satisfaction.
22. Seven steps for handling customer complaints:
    1. Listen attentively to everything the customer has to say.
    2. Ask questions that help clarify your understanding of the situation and that let the customer know you are paying serious attention.
    3. Propose a solution to the problem.
    4. Ask if the customer would be satisfied with the solution.
    5. If the solution is unsatisfactory to the customer, ask the customer what solution would be satisfactory.
    6. If the customer's solution falls within the scope of company policy and/or you have the authority to grant the solution it is best to act on the solution as quickly as possible.
    7. If the customer's solution does not conform to company policy or is not within your authority to grant, then explain the situation and take whatever steps are required to at least try to satisfy the customer.

23. Always smile with your voice when talking to a customer on the telephone.

24. Always treat a customer's telephone call as if it were a personal visit to your business. Give all callers the courteous attention they deserve.

25. Understanding and working with the differences in people (customers) can become one of the most enjoyable aspects of any job that involves customer relations.

26. Extravert customers need strong interaction with employees, while introvert customers require a low-key thoughtful approach that satisfies their *inner needs.*

27. There are four basic personality types: Thinker, Feeler, Senser, and Intuiter. In the role of customer, each type is distinctly different from the others.

28. The three basic drama roles customers play during times of conflict are: Persecutor, Victim, or Rescuer.

29. The four basic life positions that customers hold in relationship to other people are:
    1. I'm Not OK — You're OK
    2. I'm Not OK — You're Not OK
    3. I'm OK — You're Not OK
    4. I'm OK — You're OK

30. The foundation for all successful customer relations is in the *I'm OK — You're OK* attitude toward people.